MAKING DECISIONS

A Guide for Couples

David R. Leama..

Introduction by John M. Drescher

HERALD PRESS
Scottdale, Pennsylvania
Kitchener, Ontario
1979

Library of Congress Cataloging in Publication Data

Leaman, David R 1947-
Making decisions.

1. Marriage. 2. Decision-making. I. Title.
HQ734.L365 301.42 78-27153
ISBN 0-8361-1882-0 pbk.

Published simultaneously in Canada by Herald Press, Kitchener, Ont. N2G 4M5
Library of Congress Catalog Card Number: 78-27153
International Standard Book Number: 0-8361-1882-0
Printed in the United States of America
Design: Alice B. Shetler / Cover photo: H. Armstrong Roberts

10 9 8 7 6 5 4 3 2 1

MAKING DECISIONS

This book is dedicated to my loving wife, Joyce, who faithfully helps me grow emotionally and spiritually. Without her insights and perceptivity, the book would not have been completed. Joyce joined me in the writing of numerous sections of the book. I thank God for the experiences of living and working with her. Together we have learned much regarding mutual decision-making.

Contents

Introduction

In a meeting a young person stood and asked, "Anyone got a car going anywhere?" Many of us live like that. Life goes on but direction is not clear. There is no goal. Decisions are made by whatever happens to be going on. And when we lose a sense of direction and goal we become victims of circumstances. Without decisive action we turn with the tide. We are people pushed about. If we are not God-led, we are mob-led. If we do not sense God's leading, we finally react to life or take a fatalistic approach. If we are not guided by principles we will be pushed by pressures.

All of us need to make many decisions. Decisions determine direction. Decisions also can lead to delight or despair. Because this is true, we need some clear advice on making the right kind of decisions. David R. Leaman's book, *Making Decisions: A Guide for Couples,* is of real help in this important area.

All families are familiar with the struggles which making decisions can stir within us and between us. Husbands and wives as never before face decisions these days regarding where to live and what will be best for all concerned. Part of the reason for this is that we are a mobile society and the choices of where we will live and what we will do are multiplied. We need to decide what lifestyle we will adopt.

For the Christian, decision making is particularly crucial. We believe not only that we need divine guidance and that God through His Word, Spirit, and fellow Christians promises guidance, but that God wants us to discern clearly His will and that His will is always best.

Astrology and other artificial means people use to seek direction point to the need people have for help outside themselves. The great growth in such sources is a sign that people lack firsthand contact with God. If people do not sense being led by God, they will seek leading from other sources such as the stars or turn to a kind of life directed by sheer materialism.

Making Decisions: A Guide for Couples is especially helpful because it draws both from biblical and psychological perspectives. Too often these are separated. Yet brought together they can provide honest and courgeous direction for decision making. This volume conveys many helpful suggestions which, if followed, should provide satisfactory results.

A young woman approximately twenty years old came to my office for counseling. She told me that she needed to make an important decision and she wanted help to discern God's will. We talked for some time. Then I reached into my desk drawer, took out a card, and wrote three questions on it: (1) Do I believe God's will is always best? (2) Do I really want to know God's will? and (3) Will I follow His will, as He reveals it, regardless of what this may mean to me?

I handed the card to her. She pondered the statements a while in silence. Then she said, "If it were just not for that last question." Yet it's true that most of the problems in divine guidance hinge on that question. Divine guidance emerges at the center of the human will. When we commit ourselves to God's will, regardless of the consequences, light often breaks upon our path.

This book does not do away with the responsibility which God places upon our shoulders for making use of the assistance of other persons, the Scriptures, and the judgment God gives us.

Leaman lets us see the emotions which are many times experienced in our search for direction. Beyond this he provides specific guidance and shares a systematic process for helping couples make decisions. He asks us to look honestly at ourselves and our capabilities and to weigh seriously the alternative choices which are available to us. The strong thrust of the book is that God does give direction in the decisions we face.

Designed specifically with married couples in mind, *Making Decisions: A Guide for Couples* is an excellent book to ponder with your marriage partner and to keep handy for future reference. It can also be used for group study and as a resource for counselors to help others in the decision-making process.

John M. Drescher, Author
Meditations for the Newly Married, *Talking It Over*, and *Now Is the Time to Love*.

So Now What Do We Do?

The strongest principle of growth lies in human choice.

George Eliot in
Daniel Deronda

CHAPTER 1

So Now What Do We Do?

My wife and I drove through the colorful Pennsylvania mountains in silence. Though we were surrounded by God's beauty everywhere, we felt far away from His presence. We were overwhelmed by the burdensome responsibility of making a crucial decision.

Joyce finally broke the silence and asked, "What do you think we should do?"

I replied with a note of frustration and anguish, "I really don't know, but I wish God would give us some sort of sign."

I thought of the Old Testament prophets who received

unusual signs and fantastic visions that verified God's will. I reflected upon Gideon who witnessed a miracle with the sheep fleece when he felt uncertain of his responsibilities. I hoped that somehow God would favor us with some supernatural indication of what decision to make.

For four months we had been seeking a professional job opportunity in counseling psychology. We had sent letters to over 80 advertised positions at the university level and to private or state mental health clinics. Some of the positions had been filled before my application was processed. Many institutions were seeking a specialist with unique qualifications and several years' experience. It was an unusually tight year for jobs in the counseling profession. Each day I hurried to the mailbox only to find another letter which politely informed me that in some way my qualifications did not fit the institutional needs. Some institutions responded that I had too much clinical training and others indicated that I didn't have enough.

By the end of July, we began to despair and wonder what was happening to us. We both felt some anger toward God for leaving us out on a limb, especially in light of His promises to sustain and supply our daily needs. A sense of lostness had crept into our hearts.

During the four months of seeking employment, we had pondered the matter of faith a lot and had discussed it with others. We struggled with finding the balance between simply trusting God to provide the right job and actively pursuing our employment goal. The turning point came when my wife's elementary teaching contract came due. To sign would guarantee a stable income and I could probably find some part-time counseling opportunities around the university town. Besides we could continue to live in our purchased mobile home.

This solution certainly was the safest one and insured some financial security. However, it would have required that my wife continue as the primary wage earner for at least another year. Neither of us was anxious for that. Such a plan would provide very limited opportunities for meaningful and challenging counseling experiences. Futhermore, it did not demand faith or risk, but only hanging on to what we already had.

But what other alternatives were available? No job possibilities were offered to me. I had not been invited anywhere for an interview. And no evidence surfaced to suggest any change in that trend. Through prayer and fasting, in addition to sharing our concern with close friends, we decided to take a leap of faith and hold God to His promises.

It was both exciting and frightening! We had to be willing to do as the bus slogan says, "Leave the driving up to us." We'd let God do the steering.

The Saturday before the school contract was due, we advertised in the paper that our mobile home was for sale. Also we wrote a letter and sealed the envelope stating that Joyce would not be renewing her contract.

On Monday, things began to happen. At 7:30 a.m. we received a call from a university inviting me to come for a job interview. Later that week, two mental health clinics requested interviews. We were ecstatic—surprised by joy. God indeed works in amazing ways. "O the depth of the riches and wisdom and knowledge of God! How unsearchable are his judgments and how inscrutable his ways!" (Romans 11:33). We both learned in that moment a new meaning of the Scriptures, "The just shall live by faith," and "Trust in the Lord."

All three job interviews were in the East and within 350 miles of each other, enabling us to schedule all of them for the same trip. We expected God to make clear to us which job was ours by allowing me to be accepted in only one institution. However, this is where God's sense of humor comes through! All three positions were offered to me and each wanted a definite answer within seven days. It seemed that God had thrown us a curve. We had not expected a surprise package of alternatives when we prayed for God's guidance in decision-making.

After some initial reflection, we realized anew that God always allows us to experience those things that will maximize our personal growth. In His all-knowing love, He permits us to face difficult choices to enrich our lives and mold us into His likeness. Not only does God challenge our faith, but He also requires a disciplined mind and deep reflective thought in making choices conformable to His will.

Again, we wanted a special revelation—an unmistakable sign. We were tired of struggling with decisions and tired of growing. We wanted the easy way out! I even fantasized in daydreams that God would come to me in a vision and write the answer on the wall.

But God was giving us three genuine alternatives. Each job seemed to be acceptable and each had some advantages over the others. Our task was to carefully consider each alternative and make an active commitment to one. We knew the time for honest self-confrontations and the need for value clarification had only begun.

After experiencing the heavy responsibility of choosing between three acceptable alternatives, we began to realize that the struggle we try to avoid in making decisions is the very process that brings meaning and joy into one's life.

The ability to choose is the crowning joy of humanity! To choose is to grow and live. The struggle of making decisions enriches our lives and opens us to deeper reality and exciting growth. Our choices are the basis for experiencing meaning. Decision-making is a daily process that keeps us on the growing edge. Without the risks of choosing, we cannot give or receive love. If we refuse to choose, we refuse to grow and thus begin to wither and die. Choosing is an inescapable responsibility as well as an exciting privilege of life.

Anxiety and Anger in Making Decisions

I believe that God created me with a capacity to experience a whole galaxy of feelings. That the emotions that I have at any given moment are a tribute to the God who gave me such wonderful capacities to feel. And that I will know who I am and will become more and more who He made me to be only when I accept my true feelings of Him and of others.

John Powell in a workshop, "Experiments in Knowing and Being Known"

CHAPTER 2

Anxiety and Anger in Making Decisions

A little boy and his father went on a drive in the country. Becoming engrossed in their conversation, the father did not pay close attention to where they drove. Not knowing exactly where they were, the father turned onto an unmarked dirt road that he hoped would take him the right direction. After several miles of winding, the road came to an abrupt end at a huge, abandoned quarry. Realizing their plight, the boy looked to his father and said hesitantly, "Do you think God knows we're out here, Daddy?"

The little boy's question expresses what we sometimes

feel in the midst of life's demanding situations. Where do we go from here? Where is the direction I need? How often we experience mixed feelings when we have to make a difficult decision. We may feel anxious about choosing and uncertain about the consequences since we cannot control the outcomes. Everyone feels a tinge of insecurity in decision-making. Choosing between several options can be very confusing, as described by a little boy who tried to catch bees:

> I wait 'til they light on a floor, then I run up behind them with a glass jar, and the silly bee thinks the bottom of the jar is the top but it's really the bottom 'cause it's upside down and the top is on the bottom, and the bee gets all mixed up. I know just how the bee feels!

Sometimes we feel torn between alternatives because we are so keenly aware of the need to make the *right* decision. In those crucial moments, we may recognize our basic hidden feelings of inadequacy. We don't want to make a mistake and may be afraid that the choice will not fulfill our needs. The responsibility of making a wise choice may seem overwhelming.

When my wife and I were presented with the three-job opportunities, I felt bewildered and uncertain. Because of my Christian values, I wanted to please God and my wife as well as satisfy my needs. I wasn't sure that any of the alternatives would fully meet those criteria. What if the option which looked most attractive to me was not what God wanted? What if my first choice was my wife's third choice? How could we resolve the conflict without

1. Art Linkletter, *Kids Say the Darndest Things* (Englewood Cliffs, N.J.: Prentice-Hall, 1957), p. 116.

one of us feeling cheated or resentful? Part of me wanted to avoid the whole problem, while the other part wanted to make a hasty decision to get it off my mind. Somehow it seemed impossible that one option could mutually satisfy both my wife's needs and mine and be congruent with God's will.

In that moment, I felt alone. I was reluctant to discuss the dilemma with Joyce for fear of influencing her to see things my way. God was silent and I felt the weight of choosing rested heavily on my shoulders.

"Why don't you show me Your way? You know that I love You and want to do Your will," I prayed. "But what is Your will for me in this case? Should I just go ahead and select an alternative and expect my wife to be submissive and follow? What about her feelings?"

How could we make a mutual decision that would meet both our needs? What did God really expect from me in this situation?

I remember driving in silence with all these questions racing through my mind. I wanted my wife and I to be in unity and both of us content with the decision. I had seen too many couples in which one partner made the major decision and the other agreed but inwardly resented it and felt estranged.

As I pondered for the next few days I found myself asking repeatedly, "Why doesn't God make His will known and why did He place me in this position in the first place?" I began to get angry and question God's love. How could He do this to me? What was He trying to prove, anyhow? Beneath the anger was a "should." God *should* tell me what to do! After all, He tells us to pray and promises hundreds of times in the Scripture that He will reveal His will. Yet, He remained silent.

One morning in sheer frustration, I released my anger toward God. With fist-pounding and tears, I expressed my feelings of being neglected and mistreated. I told Him He shouldn't be acting that way toward me. After exploding and shouting at God, I sat down in silence with remorse and contemplation. As I got in touch with my feelings, I began to realize that my anger developed from a demand that God, the Sovereign Creator and Lord, answer me in the way I expected. I wanted God to meet my puny expectations in my time framework. I felt He was unfair because He wasn't meeting me on my terms.

I felt foolish and ashamed when I recognized my arrogance. When I confessed my hostility and set aside my demands, I became free to hear God's voice and receive His guidance.

I learned several important things from these experiences. First, when God was temporarily silent, my emotions intensified and I got a more honest picture of my basic humanity. Initially, I felt anxiety which turned into a selfish demand and anger toward God. I recognized that at the core of my being I was selfish and needed God's grace.

Another principle I realized was that God's silence is a powerful way to test my faith. God confronted me with the question, "Will you trust Me?" I had to learn to surrender my feelings to God and discover again the deep truth of the Scripture, "Be still and know that I am God." Without these experiences, my faith would become stale. Because God loves me He allowed me to experience dilemmas as a tool to fashion me into the likeness of Christ and to help me grow into a more whole person.

Since emotions play such a key part in decision-making, perhaps my wife's thoughts and feelings during the time of our decision-making regarding the job may be helpful:

During the time of decision-making about David's job, I felt angry and resentful. After all, I had been the one who had to sacrifice my career so we could move and David could enter the doctoral program in the first place. With a feeling of desperation I wondered, "Will *my* needs never be met? Will my desires always be squelched so that he can do his own thing?" Loneliness set in. "Don't I count in this relationship except to be the breadwinner for three years and now I'm of no significance?"

There also was a sense of strangulation. Here I was caught in the middle between feeling a responsibility toward my parents and a love so deep for my husband that I wanted to do what was the best thing for him. I couldn't express that to him, for the fear that he would choose on the basis of my needs alone and then later find it to be the wrong choice for *him*. I couldn't live with that kind of guilt! Traveling along the highway between interviews, I remember turning my head and pretending to look at the scenery so that my husband wouldn't see the tears of frustration rolling down my face as I tried to keep all these emotions inside.

Then I became keenly aware that God didn't seem to be anywhere near us in this turmoil. Had He abandoned me too? Didn't He promise that He would never leave us or desert us? It sure didn't *feel* that way! FEELINGS!

That was it! I had been relying on my feelings, *not* my faith in God!

"Lord, forgive me! But, Lord, what if I do turn all of this over to You? What if You require something of me I don't want to give? Lord, that's risky!"

A still small voice reminded me to be confident of this very thing, "that he which hath begun a good work in you will perform it until the day of Jesus Christ." (Philippians 1:6). It was true. God had called us into the doctoral program. There was no doubt about that. He had brought us through it, had provided for us, cared for us, and loved us through peak and valley experiences. He would do it now if I would let Him.

He was calling me to put *all* my emotions in His hands, to let Him handle them, to trust Him. After all, wasn't this the essence of the faith that I shared with others? Now was the time to put my words into action in my own life!

Fear and Guilt in Making Decisions

For God has said, "I will never, never *fail you nor forsake you." That is why we can say without any doubt or fear, "The Lord is my Helper and I am not afraid of anything that mere man can do to me!"*

Hebrews 13: 5,6,
Living Bible

CHAPTER 3

Fear and Guilt in Making Decisions

Emotions are an essential part of our humanity. They play a crucial role in the decisions we make. Emotions may contribute positively to effective choosing or they may prevent us from making successful decisions. Perhaps the two most inhibiting emotions are fear and guilt.

Fear

Fear is a common emotion that people experience in decision-making. The greatest fear is a fear of failure. If, for example, an individual judges himself according to a stringent, moralistic standard and has a demanding, perfectionistic attitude, he may experience fear in decision-making. Why? At the basis of his decisions is the fear of failing or making a mistake in his choice—a fear that he may not perform according to his expectations.

Richard Beery has explained fear of failure in the following manner:

> The individual seems to start with the assumption that "my ability must be very high (brilliant) to be adequate; if it's anything else, I'm dumb, stupid, incompetent."
>
> . . . My belief is that the problem arises from an internal assumption that one's personal worth is contingent on one's ability. . . .
>
> . . . If individuals have come to believe that they must possess an extremely high level of ability to be okay, to be worthwhile, and that anything less is tantamount to stupidity and makes them worthless, then any kind of evaluative situation is, naturally, going to be extremely threatening.[1]

Thus, underlying the fear of failure is the hidden assumption that a person's worth is somehow tied to one's ability. Ability is reflected in performance. Since society often teaches people that the level of ability and talents is the basis of worth and acceptance, the fear of failure becomes a fear that others may not approve. The person who needs constant approval from others to feel worthwhile is in a miserable bondage. Since he cannot accept himself realistically, he is tossed about by the wishes of others. The fear of disapproval from persons who are important in his life incapacitates and paralyzes

1. Richard Beery, "Fear of Failure in the Student Experience," *The Personnel and Guidance Journal*, Vol. 54, Dec., 1975, p. 200.

him. The tragedy is that the fear of disapproval is kept alive because no decision pleases everyone. Somebody will react with disapproval.

Trapped by these irrational demands, one is not free to grow and choose realistically. The insidious and irrational beliefs behind the fear sound like this: "My worth and value as a human depends upon my abilities. I am worthless and unlovable if I do not perform according to my expectations. I cannot be loved or valued unless I prove that I have remarkable abilities. If I make a mistake, I am worthless and no good. I must be perfectly right in order to be loved."

Cecil Osborne states,

> We must not expect perfection of ourselves or of others. Generalized perfectionism is often the result of overcompensating for feelings of weakness or inadequacy or of perfectionistic parents who demanded the ultimate in performance. Fearing the judgment of such parents, the child usually reacts by striving to please and tries to reach all of the goals set for him.[2]

For example, a woman named Fran confided through heavy tears that the main reason she went into the convent was to prove to herself and God that she was acceptable and worthwhile. Her father was a demanding, insensitive man who seldom gave her positive feedback. No matter what she did, he would coldly say, "You could have done better." For years, she struggled to please him, but was not given the satisfaction that her performance was acceptable. Fran was never "good enough"

2. Cecil Osborn, *Release from Fear and Anxiety* (Waco, Tex.: Word Books, 1976), p. 99

in her parents' eyes. She never really felt loved. In exasperation, she entered into a monastic life where she fervently dedicated her energy to service for others. She felt compelled to show God that she was worthy of love, yet deep inside she was afraid. She became acutely aware of her weakness.

Fran's fears grew. She had frequent nightmares and dreams that God was saying to her, "You are not good enough to love." Fran's fear became so intense that she was not able to meet the service requirements of the convent. In desperation, she entered counseling with this confession, "I am afraid—afraid to live and afraid to die. If I live, I am a failure. If I die, I am condemned."

Fran later experienced the beautiful freedom in Christianity when she realized that God loves us as we are and His grace covers all our inadequacies.

The fearful person demands exceptional performance, but painfully realizes that he cannot meet the demands. He attempts to cover up his inadequacies. He may try to avoid making decisions since it is easier to procrastinate than to face the risks of choosing. Rather than put his abilities on the line he will quit before starting. This is often the case with students who are underachievers and refuse to put forth conscientious effort. It is not a lack of motivation but a fear of failure that prevents them from performing sufficiently. Ironically, the fear of failure produces failure. Fear has a strange magnetism! It is like a self-fulfilling prophecy. The more we fear that something terrible is going to happen to us, the more we increase the probability of its occurrence. It seems that we become our fears. When we fear something intensely, we are captives to it and may bring devastating consequences upon ourselves.

A man developed a strong fear that he would lose his job. He became overly cautious and extremely sensitive to his mistakes. He became more suspicious and judgmental of others. His anxiety increased and interfered with his performance. Four months later, he was fired from his job.

A woman feared that she would have to undergo a hysterectomy before age 30. In her late twenties, she developed severe cramps in the abdominal area and excessive distress during menstruation. Though doctors verified that no physical disability existed, the symptoms persisted and worsened. Soon after her twenty-ninth birthday, she was taken to the hospital and a hysterectomy was performed.

Trying to run away from our fears may propel us headlong into the very experience which we fear. Attempts to avoid facing our inadequacies and hiding our fears are always emotionally devastating. Avoidance only intensifies the fear.

Fear in decision-making may also stem from a subtle anxiety about becoming a more responsible person. To choose wisely requires a willingness to change, which may result in more responsibility. A noted author wrote:

> Some individuals avoid finding out more about themselves for fear of having to give up a self with which they have grown comfortable or "satisfied." Most people have an initial inclination to resist personal change anyway, but this resistance is even stronger for a person who cannot "fit" new or changed behavior into his current concept of self . . . Other individuals are reluctant to find out more about themselves because of the threat of having to change in the direction of being more personally mature. . . . Greater

maturity means greater responsibility and for some this is a frightening possibility.[3]

The Bible gives hope to the fearful. Confront the fear and you will discover that fear loses its hold. As the beloved apostle puts it, "Perfect love casts out fear" (1 John 4:18). This great truth has been demonstrated many times and results in emotional wholeness. Accepting God's infinite love for us and claiming the truth enables us to face our fears and frees us from their bondage. We can learn to accept ourselves with our inadequacies and failures.

Bruce Larson, in a powerful book, *Living on the Growing Edge*,[4] described several factors to consider that will minimize the power of fear in our lives:

Analyze the fear. Recognize the source of the fear and consider if it is realistic or irrational. A realistic fear is one that involves an apparent external threat, while irrational fear is grounded in submerged motivations without a solid external basis. Accept the realistic fears and commit them to God.

Don't fight an irrational fear. Rather than resist the fear, face it; for the more you fight the fear, the more you increase its power over you. Victor Frankl, with logotherapy techniques, emphasizes the importance of exaggerating the area of weakness or the object that is feared. If you can't sleep, rather than trying to sleep, try to stay awake as long as you can—and you will discover

3. Don E. Hamacheck, *Encounters with Self* (New York: Holt, Rinehart, and Winston, 1971), p. 2.

4. Bruce Larson, *Living on the Growing Edge* (Grand Rapids, Mich.: Zondervan, 1968).

that sleep overtakes you. If you stutter, instead of resisting it, try to stutter as much as you possibly can and your problem is likely to dissipate.

Be willing to risk failure. Everyone has a right to make mistakes. Live by faith and exercise your privilege to choose. Remember that God loves us regardless of our performance.

Recognize fear as faith in reverse. Do the thing you fear and you will find that you are acting in faith. In Christ, we are free to fail, for the Scriptures teach that the believer has no condemnation and is without blame in His eyes.

Guilt

In spite of our good intentions and efforts, we do make mistakes. We make inappropriate and wrong choices. Thus decision-making is sometimes laden with guilt feelings. Guilt feelings develop from our evaluations about behaviors we have committed. After a decision is made and action initiated, we analyze and judge the action according to an internalized set of standards. We make conclusions—realistic or irrational—about our personhood by evaluating our performance in light of our standards. We may view ourselves as bad and unacceptable to God and others. We may conclude that we are unlovable and worthless. We may even alienate others through our negative attitudes about ourselves.

For example, when Mary evaluated all her commitments and chose not to carry through on the idea of starting a ladies' Bible study group at her house, her friends were disappointed. After telling them all of her decision, she began to feel guilty. She thought that perhaps she had made the wrong decision; that somehow she should have been able to squeeze the Bible study into the week's schedule. Because of her self-blame, she anticipated that her friends would condemn and reject her also. So she avoided them. Even when the friends approached her, Mary was caustic, abrupt, and rude. Her negative behavior alienated them. This led to more guilt feelings, followed by self-condemnation with increased withdrawal and loneliness.

Guilt may become an incredibly consuming emotion which manipulates everything and everyone around itself. Some people, like Mary, spend a tremendous amount of useless energy attacking themselves for mistakes or wrong choices. Guilt feelings lead to a pathetic "pity party" in which their whole world revolves around guilt. The greater the self-condemnation, the greater the self-pity. They become wrapped up in an empty, isolated world, shutting others out because they feel so unworthy. They desperately try to remedy the discomfort by punishing themselves.

In the case of Mary, the more she focused on the guilt feelings, the more self-centered she became and the more loneliness and unhappiness resulted. The vicious cycle can easily be recognized. First we make a mistake or do wrong and experience guilt feelings. Then we condemn and punish ourselves, alienate others, experience estrangement from God, all of which produces loneliness and leads to more inappropriate behavior, followed by more guilt feelings.

Are Your Guilt Feelings Irrational?

The basis for guilt feelings may be realistic or irrational. One may not only feel guilty about an immoral act, but also may feel guilty simply because he or she did not perform according to his expectations. Irrational guilt feelings stem from striving for unattainable goals.

Albert Ellis, a contemporary psychotherapist, has developed a very practical theory that unhappiness and problem behavior stems from the irrational beliefs a person upholds. Some irrational assumptions that are likely to induce guilt feelings and are related to our sense of inadequacy include:[5]

> *Irrational Idea 1* is that it is a dire necessity for an adult to be loved or approved by almost everyone for virtually everything he does.
>
> *Irrational Idea 2* is that one should be thoroughly competent, adequate, and achieving in all possible respects.
>
> *Irrational Idea 3* is that it is catastrophic if perfect solutions to the grim realities of life are not immediately found.

The central theme of the above statements is that the erroneous beliefs to which people cling lead to unhappiness. They are assumptions which are taught by society, in a negative way, through lack of parental love and, also, through cultural expectations. They are impossible goals to which people unnecessarily cling.

Check yourself. Look closely at the source of your guilt feelings and determine if you unwittingly hold to some irrational misconceptions. Ask yourself these questions: Do I feel "guilty" when someone disagrees with my ideas? Do I feel guilty when people don't like my performance? Do I feel guilty when I say "no" to a request? Is the approval of others more important to me than standing up for what I feel and believe? If your answer is

---

5. Albert Ellis and Robert A. Harper, *A New Guide to Rational Living* Englewood Cliffs, N.J.: Prentice-Hall, 1975, pp. 79, 92, and 163.

"yes" to most of these questions, then you probably are holding onto Irrational Idea 1.

How about Irrational Idea 2? Do you subtly expect that you should be thoroughly competent in everything you do? Do you have an unrealistic demanding attitude of perfectionism? If you do, you are probably experiencing a perplexing sense of "guilt" and inadequate feelings. Do you tolerate mistakes in yourself? Is it okay to fail? When you make a mistake do you become miserable to live with and blame others?

What happens when things don't go your way? What happens if you can't find a complete solution to a problem? Do you feel worthless when your decisions need to be changed? Honestly check your attitudes and see if they reflect some irrational assumptions. Such misconceptions could be detrimental to effective decision-making.

Paul Tournier distinguishes realistic guilt from irrational guilt feelings in the following manner:

> . . . the true guilt of men comes from the things with which they are reproached by God in their innermost hearts. Only they can discover what these things are. And they are usually very different from the things with which they are reproached by men.[6]

He further elaborates that "true" guilt is disobedience to God or not depending on God alone. ("You shall have no other gods before me." Exodus 20:3.) Unrealistic guilt or "false" guilt emerges from breaking internalized social standards which may not have any biblical basis.

6. Paul Tournier, *Guilt and Grace* (New York: Harper and Row, 1962), p. 67.

A realistic basis for guilt is the violation of the law of love—a refusal to love God with your whole being and love your neighbor as yourself (Matthew 22:34-40). Realistic guilt is related to refusal to recognize God as Creator and live in dependence upon Him. It is also the awareness that you did not act consistently with your personal beliefs. Guilt is present when your action violates your value system, or your conduct is not in agreement with the values you espouse. When you state the golden rule as your maxim, but act in any way different from that sacrificial love principle, you sin and incur guilt, and your awareness of that wrong is experienced as realistic guilt feelings.

Realistic guilt feelings can be a valuable experience. They confront us with the truth and motivate us into proper action. The presence of realistic guilt feelings is the work of God in our lives, the action of His truth confronting our error, making us aware of our wrong. When we sin we are guilty, and guilt feelings are the consequences of transgressing God's laws. Those painful guilt feelings and the deep remorse for doing wrong can be the impetus to move us into constructive action. Realistic guilt feelings can be the catalyst which stimulates us to amend broken relationships with God and man.

What purpose do irrational guilt feelings serve? Why do people allow them to exist? Is there a subtle security in maintaining such guilt feelings? Yes! Irrational guilt feelings block people from relating honestly to others and God. They are a way of showing others that you are "not worthy" of their love. If you are "not worthy" of their love, then you don't have to be responsible to return love. Holding to irrational guilt feelings becomes a way to avoid growth and change. You can use the guilt feelings to protect yourself from intimacy and becoming vulnerable. Irrational guilt feelings may, therefore, be a manipulative tool that excuses you from exercising responsibility and love.

Guilt as a Motive for Choosing

Guilt can be the primary motivating factor in some decisions. People may make decisions because they feel guilty about an action they have taken or a thought they experienced. Making decisions on this basis is a way of saying, "I'm sorry, please forgive me."

An example of a decision based on guilt feelings is the case of Fred. He was the father of three children. All the family members wanted to go on a Saturday picnic. Fred wanted to golf. The family argued and fought about it all Friday night. Fred won out and went golfing, even though some of the children cried and whimpered. His wife was hurt and disappointed but he insisted that he seldom gets a chance to play in a local golf tourney and he deserved the break. That next week, he bought some token gifts for each family member and some roses for his wife. When he honestly explored his motives, he stated, "I did it because I felt guilty and I wanted to make up for it."

A mother felt guilty for spanking her child, so she permitted him to stay up late and gave him several special privileges to absolve her feelings.

A son volunteered to clean the house and wash windows at home on Saturday aftenoon because he felt guilty for coming home drunk on Friday night.

Decisions motivated by guilt feelings are misleading and deceitful. The action may "appear good" but in reality it is unsatisfactory and sometimes repulsive. Choosing and acting from guilt is also terribly confusing to the other person involved because, unfortunately, guilt-motivated actions are sometimes labeled "love." Partners may spend a lifetime making up to each other. Like penance, the person pays the debt for the previous wrongdoings committed in the relationship. Both persons expect it. They may do things for each other not because of open genuine love and honesty, but because they feel they owe it. They are motivated by guilt feelings, each owing good deeds to the other, paying back the debts from previous interactions. Such relationships are tragic and devoid of personal fulfillment.

As we carefully observe the motives in decision-making, we may recognize the presence of guilt more frequently than we want to admit. When guilt is a motivating factor, it is tied to certain values or assumptions we uphold. Thus the process of analyzing our beliefs and clarifying the values is crucial to avoid making choices on the basis of guilt feelings. The "shoulds" by which we live need to be honestly challenged to see if they stem from irrational assumptions or are grounded upon solid biblical principles.

Biblical Methods for Coping with Guilt

Only an approach which includes the spiritual dimension of man can adequately give a complete solution to the problem of guilt. The Scriptures teach that true moral guilt exists. Our entire society operates under the belief that objective guilt is indeed a fact and that men violate meaningful laws. Every individual in honest moments recognizes that he or she is guilty of breaking the moral law. Everyone is in error. All have sinned (Romans

3:19-23). Everyone is objectively guilty morally and at various times subjectively experiences guilt feelings. The biblical approach deals with both aspects of guilt whereas other methods focus entirely upon the subjective realm.

The following steps are essential in effectively coping with guilt feelings:

1. *Recognize and own your guilt feelings.* Ownership of guilt is to say honestly, "I took a particular action at that time because I desired to do it." Take full responsibility for your wrong choice. Accept your mistake—your sin—realistically. This perhaps is the hardest task because as humans we constantly struggle to make ourselves appear good. Admitting mistakes, owning our wrong choices, is simply accepting our humanity. When we honestly accept our humanity, we open the door for wholeness and freedom. Admit your error to yourself.

2. *Recognize and analyze the source of guilt (Psalm 32).* Is your guilt emerging from some irrational assumption? Are you expecting perfection of yourself or reaching for an impossible goal? Is the guilt feeling some disguised form of basic inadequacy, or does it stem from some specific objective action that was morally wrong? Locate the source of the guilt and see if it comes from a violation of the law of love or an inability to perform according to someone's expectations.

3. *Confront your irrational guilt feelings and confirm your worth.* Criticize your irrational beliefs. Pick them apart. Analyze the grounds for your assumptions. See if there is any biblical basis for the assumptions you hold. Are your assumptions valid or have you simply incorporated them from your parents or society? Remind yourself that you are human and thus you make both

good and bad choices. God has formed you from the womb and you are something special (Psalm 139:14-18). God says you are extremely worthwhile because you exist as His creation (Isaiah 43:5-8). You are God's workmanship (Ephesians 2:10). Jesus further emphasized your worth by dying for you on the cross. As God's creation you have infinite worth; as a human you are loved by God. Your worth is not based upon performance but upon existence. God loves you and has a unique and exciting plan for your life.

4. *Confess your realistic guilt to God (1 John 1:9; 2 Chronicles 7:14, 15).* State specifically what sin you committed, take ownership for it, and repent. Confession means to agree with God that you are guilty of transgressing the law, to admit to the accusation of the law. This allows no room for making excuses or using defenses. It requires simple honesty. To repent means to decide to change. Repentance involves a recognition of wrong and the responsibility to change the action (change of purpose).

The forgiveness of God is available to everyone who confesses his sin. God is compassionate and merciful. God is willing to forgive and cleanse *every* individual of *every* sin simply on the grounds of genuine repentance and confession.

Andrew Murray points out several beautiful concepts regarding cleansing.[7] Cleansing refers to being washed and set free from the pollution of sin. Cleansing removes our sense of defilement and feelings of impurity. Thus cleansing pertains to our subjective guilt feelings and

---

7. Andrew Murray, *The Power of the Blood of Jesus* (Old Tappan, N.J.: Revell, 1974).

washes away our degrading sense of being dirty and worthless. In the Old Testament, the offerings pertained to the removal of the objective moral guilt (forgiveness of sin) but cleansings were for the conditions that occurred as a result of sin. Offerings were substitutionary, but cleansing was done to the person and in the person's body. In cleansing, the person could feel the experience of being washed.

Thus, cleansing refers to the removal of guilt feelings, the sense of impurity and worthlessness. The impact of God's cleansing is that when we confess, we can visualize God washing us completely clean and we have no grounds for a guilty conscience. All grounds for self-condemnation are removed. We do not need to be aware of past sins, for we are cleansed and pronounced by God as "not guilty." God views the believer as righteous!

Thus, confession not only means to agree with God that we sinned, but also to agree with God that we are cleansed completely. If we accept this truth, we have no reason whatsoever to condemn ourselves and feel guilty upon confession.

5. *Accept by faith God's cleansings. Act in faith by making new choices and reevaluating your goals.* By accepting God's forgiveness we are free from condemnation and guilt feelings. We are free to leave the past behind and go forward. We are free to receive love and give love. We are free to choose and be chosen. The wrong decisions we make never incapacitate us from making other more meaningful decisions. We only incapacitate ourselves by wallowing in guilt feelings. Let us appropriate God's forgiveness and press toward the goal of serving Him honestly and without fear.

A Decision-Making Plan for Couples

Our mind must be like a parachute. The latter opens up; if it does not, it isn't any good. Likewise, we must open our eyes and minds to new truths. We must hunger and thirst after new truth and new knowledge, enabling us to soar aloft above our problems on the wings of faith and understanding.

Joseph Murphy in
Believe in Yourself

CHAPTER 4

A Decision-Making Plan for Couples

In this chapter, I share a decision-making model designed to help couples choose between two or more definite alternatives. The model is both practical and stimulating. My wife and I, along with other couples, have found it helpful on numerous occasions. The model is especially valuable when a major decision must be made which will significantly affect the lives of the couple. The model will help the couple identify their values and needs in light of each alternative and select the option that best fulfills the personal needs of each person.

The process of decision-making by couples is complex because two people bring to the relationship two different sets of values with a varying degree of overlap. Not only are the value systems unique, but the style or approach to making decisions is different. Both individuals must be actively involved in making a choice together if the results are to be gratifying and meaningful. One partner cannot permit his or her values to be squelched or not considered without feeling hurt, alienated, and angry. A couple relationship in which one parter always chooses and the other always follows, is likely to be a stunted and unfulfilling relationship. Decision-making by couples must include mutual involvement and bargaining in order for the interaction to be fulfilling. The needs and values of each person must be expressed and considered carefully.

Two unique value systems must be harmonized to form a mutual decision. Joint decision-making necessarily entails bargaining. Obviously not all the values of one partner can be satisfied all the time. A mutual agreement must be made in which each partner recognizes and accepts the reality that some of his or her values will be ungratified in any particular decision. Each must be willing to consider the other's needs and bargain together in good faith.

This is hard to do since we are basically selfish creatures! We want decisions to go our way and we frequently manipulate others, however subtly, to get what we want. At least two erroneous beliefs inhibit people from utilizing a mutual decision-making approach. First, we are afraid that our needs won't be met and the partner will take advantage of us. Therefore, we cling to our position and protect our "rights." Afraid of being cheated and that our needs will be unmet, we become inflexible and narrow insisting that we won't "give in" to anybody. Thus, we become blind to our partner's needs and feelings and make mutual bargaining impossible.

A second problem is that we view our beliefs and methods of doing things as superior. We look upon our partner's approach as inferior and insist that our way is better. Even some things as silly as how to squeeze—or roll—the toothpaste tube can be a source of continuing tension between partners. Neither one will ever successfully demonstrate to the other that one way of doing this is better than the other. Unless the partners agree to bargain, the arguments will continue indefinitely. Often we look upon our partner's values and needs as inferior and try to convince him or her to adopt our views and do it our way. We need to recognize that a fulfilling decision will be a blend of both persons' ideas and values.

The differences between spouses should not be looked upon as marks of inferiority but only as differences in what one has learned. Each has come from a unique family system and brings to the marriage a set of unique values. One set is not necessarily better or superior to the other. My way is not necessarily better than my wife's way nor vice versa. Because she has some different values does not mean that she is inadequate or less healthy than me. It only means that we are different and that is what makes an exciting, growing relationship possible.

Therefore, decision-making in marriage involves mutual bargaining in which the combined values of both partners are represented. Reaching a mutual agreement means that both unique value systems are considered carefully and a new value system emerges from their combination. The new value system represents the unity of two different people and their individual beliefs. The new value structure represents the gratification of both persons. It is the point of unity in which two separate individuals merge their personal needs and compromise to achieve mutual satisfaction.

When I was finally offered three job opportunities, we were faced with the dilemma of choosing the one that would most satisfy our needs. One option was especially attractive to me from a professional aspect, but that alternative was least desirable to Joyce. I knew which option she wanted but I did not understand clearly her reasons nor did I appreciate the intensity of her feelings about it. As we discussed the issues, it became clear that each of us felt the other didn't really understand his or her position. However, neither wanted to pressure the other into making the decision. I was hesitant to select my first choice knowing that she would be disappointed and perhaps resentful. She felt the same way about me. So many issues were involved that the choice seemed overwhelmingly complex.

During the seven days in which we had to make the decision, we applied a systematic decision-making model. The model developed out of our personal needs. The basic steps, and many of the exercises in each step, we shared together and discovered to be helpful in clarifying our decision and enriching our relationship with each other.

We believe that decision-making can be an exciting process when we apply a systematic approach congruent with scriptural principles. Jesus recognized the need for a disciplined approach in decision-making as illustrated in Luke 14:28-31:

> For which of you, desiring to build a tower, does not first sit down and count the cost, whether he has enough to complete it? Otherwise, when he has laid a foundation, and is not able to finish, all who see it begin to mock him, saying, "This man began to build, and was not able to finish." Or what king, going to encounter another king in war, will not sit down first and take counsel whether he is able with ten thousand to meet him who comes against him with twenty thousand?

What attracts me in the words of Jesus is the principle, "*Sit down and count the cost . . . sit down first and take counsel.*"

When facing a major decision I want to "sit" on my experience for a while. This means that I deliberately take time to reflect, to think carefully and ponder the issues, instead of making a snap decision and taking quick action. It also implies allowing my thoughts and feelings to settle. When I sit and contemplate I become familiar with my inner being and aware of my deeper feelings so that I can accept who I am and prepare to confront the issues related to the choice. Sitting and reflecting is an excellent tool for creative brooding and discovering truth, as well as for receiving divine guidance.

After the sitting experience comes the "counting process." To count involves calculation and extreme mental alertness. I can "count" accurately only when I am sufficiently relaxed and "tuned in" to personal awareness. Counting is a planned and disciplined process. It involves clarifying values, evaluating alternatives, considering the reward/cost factors, determining the risk elements, and selecting an option. During the stage of counting the cost, the input from others is extremely valuable. Not one of us is capable of consistently making wise decisions without the consultation and support of others. We must be teachable and seek assistance from others.

In this simple illustration, Jesus lays down the backbone of successful decision-making. "Sit down, count the cost, and take counsel." Let us look more carefully at these processes to develop a mutual decision-making model.

Effective decision-making involves several important elements which can be understood in sequential steps. Each phase involves exercises for the couple to do together which are designed to increase knowledge of one another and shed light on the decision to be made. Since each couple is unique and each decision is different, some of the steps and exercises may be more appropriate than others. It is not reasonable that a couple should complete every exercise. The couples may select those exercises in each phase that are most relevant. Some couples may also find that sharing the experiences with trusted friends will be meaningful and beneficial.

Here is a simple outline of the phases involved in mutual decision-making which we will consider together in the balance of this chapter:

I. Awareness of Self
   A. Relax and Contemplate
   B. Identify Relevant Concerns
   C. Acknowledge Your Feelings

II. Clarification of Personal Values
   A. Align Values with Scriptural Principles
   B. Clarify General Values

C. Identify Specific Values Related to Your Decision
D. Establish a Mutual Value System

III. Selection of Alternatives
A. Consider Pertinent Information
B. Evaluate the Alternatives
C. Analyze the Risk and Reward/Cost Factors

IV. Commitment to the Decision
A. Consider Priorities and Time
B. Accept and Act on the Choice

Awareness of Self

To be aware means to "tune in" or direct our energies and concentration on a specific object. Self-awareness involves giving careful attention to our feelings, our bodies, and our attitudes. The choices we make reflect the degree to which we understand ourselves. The more self-awareness, the better our decisions are likely to be.

A. *Relax and Contemplate*

Exercise 1. Find a quiet place where you can be alone and undisturbed. Sit comfortably or lie on your back and take in three very deep breaths. As you breathe out say the word "relax" and allow yourself to feel the calm, relaxing feelings. Continue to breathe evenly and deeply while focusing on the relaxing feelings for several minutes. Do not rush but simply allow yourself to enjoy the relaxation.

Then picture a warm ray of light from heaven entering into your body, massaging and soothing every muscle. Picture Jesus in His splendor and humility walking toward you. See His bright compassionate eyes, His strong form, His face full of understanding and wisdom. As He walks toward you, you are aware that He knows the emotional struggle you have about making the decision.

Jesus looks at you, smiles, calls you by name and says, "Your heavenly Father already knows perfectly well [what your needs are] . . . and he will give them to you if you give him first place in your life and live as he wants you to. So don't be anxious about tomorrow. God will take care of your tomorrow too. Live one day at a time" (Matthew 6:33, 34, *Living Bible*). Let yourself feel the presence of Jesus and experience His comforting words.

Exercise 2. Consider your most common style of decision-making. Look at the list of paired opposites and rate yourself on each simple scale according to your usual approach to making decisions. Later you may enjoy sharing it with your spouse.

fast . . . . slow
feeling . . . . factual
intuitive . . . . impulsive
calculated . . . . spontaneous
relaxed . . . . anxious
thinking-oriented . . . . action-oriented
indifferent . . . . overly concerned
self-sufficient . . . . dependent on others
procrastinate/delay . . . . eager initiative

Exercise 3. Sit alone in a quiet place. Reflect over past experiences in your life and consider the ways in which God has provided your needs. Write down some specific incidences in which you felt God's presence or recognized His loving intervention in your life.

Exercise 4. With your partner try writing a simple

prayer together that expresses your needs and feelings about the decision you have to make. Be sure to include a phrase of thanks or praise.

Exercise 5. Discuss with your partner the areas you have been most successful in in decision making. Observe who usually makes the decisions in your family and how they are finalized.

B. Identify Relevant Concerns

Exercise 1. With your partner, identify what each of you believes is the specific issue requiring a decision. Write it out as clearly as possible in specific terms.

You may want to complete one or more of the following phrases:

The decision we must make together is—

The goal we want to accomplish is—

The specific alternatives that I see available to us include—

Exercise 2. With your partner, list the factors and events that led up to and produced the situation. As you write them down, share the meaning that those experiences have for you.

Exercise 3. If your parents were in your shoes, what would they do? Discuss the differences in the way both sets of parents would view the dilemma. Note how similar your attitudes are to your own parents. Be sure to recognize the differences only as differences, not marks of inferiority.

C. Acknowledge Your Feelings

Acknowledge your feelings about the decision. Get in touch with your inner concerns and admit feelings of fear, anger, or guilt.

Exercise 1. Visualize yourself experiencing one of the alternatives. Walk slowly through it in your imagination. Let yourself feel what it is like to be in that situation. Imagine your spouse in that situation. What would he/she be feeling? Share your observations and perceptions with your spouse.

Exercise 2. What is the thing you fear most about the decision? What is your partner's greatest concern about the decision?

Exercise 3. If you feel some tinge of anger about the choice, locate the source and identify the demand underneath it. Ask these questions:

Is my anger related to revenge or a desire to get back at my partner?

Am I using anger to manipulate my partner into doing what I want? To get into touch with the source and demands of anger, complete the following:

"I get angry when . . ."
". . . and my behavior is . . ."
". . . and afterward I feel . . ."
". . . What I really want is . . ."[1]

Exercise 4. Are you feeling guilty over an important decision you made? List some of the "shoulds" or "should nots" you violated. How are the guilt feelings presently affecting your relationship with God and your partner? Try to apply the principles given in Scripture: 1 John 1:9 and Romans 8:31-39.

Exercise 5. If you disagree with a decision your partner has made, how do you let him or her know your feelings?

---

1. David W. Augsburger, *The Love-Fight* (Scottdale, Pa.: Herald Press, 1973), p. 55.

Clarification of Personal Values

Decisions are based upon what we value. Each choice is made according to our values and is a result of acting on what we believe is most important in our lives at that moment. Values include our perception of personal needs and what we desire for personal satisfaction. Our interests are also an extension of what we value. Every decision is made because we perceive a particular action as the option which will most satisfy what we value. The things we value the most have the greatest influence on the decisions we make.

Many of our unhappy experiences in decision-making stem from not clarifying our values carefully. We frequently suppress an important value in order to satisfy another one, only to discover later that the suppressed value was more significant than we had realized. What we believe we "ought" to do is often not what we want or even need to do. Making a decision because "we ought to" without exploring our feelings about it or considering honestly if it is best for our personal growth can be a devastating mistake. Value clarification is an extremely important experience. Methods for clarifying what we believe to be most important are varied. No one approach is all inclusive or always effective. However, any workable approach involves a careful, systematic process for considering what one believes and needs.

A. Align Values with Scriptural Principles

Exercise 1. Is there any passage in Scripture specifically related to the decision you are making? If so, read it together and discuss the implications. Are any of the alternatives you are considering not in agreement with scriptural teaching?

Exercise 2. The primary goal of every Christian as revealed in Scripture should be to glorify God through loving and obeying God. Consider the following questions and discuss them with fellow believers: Are you aware of anything in a given alternative that might hinder you from fulfilling that goal? Would Jesus be disappointed if you selected a given alternative you are considering?

If each of the alternatives is in agreement with Scriptures or does not violate the teachings of God's Word, then you can proceed to further clarify your values in terms of your personal needs and interests.

B. Clarify General Values

Exercise 1. Each of you draw a large shield and divide it into four equal parts. The shield represents important values to which you adhere and identify. After completing the exercise below, share your shield with your partner.

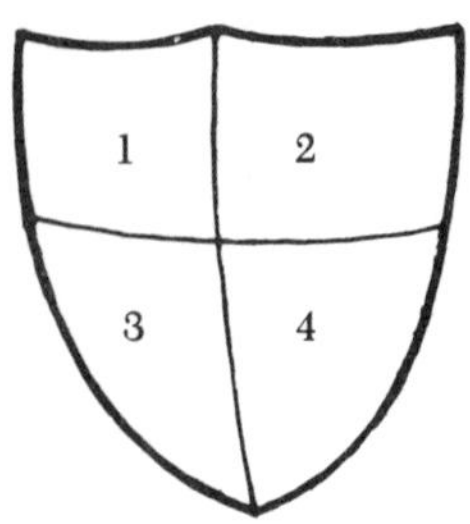

(a) In Block 1: Write down two beliefs in which you would never budge.

(b) In Block 2: In a brief sentence, write a personal motto by which you live.

(c) In Block 3: Represent symbolically by color and shape the gift you would desire most to receive from each person in your family. This could be a material item or some personal attribute you desire to have in your life.

(d) In Block 4: Write down three things you learned from your parents about making decisions. These could be things you observed or things they taught you directly.

Exercise 2. Draw a large STOP sign. Inside, write at least three things you believe you should stop doing in order to improve your relationship with your partner.

Draw a YIELD sign and write down at least three areas that you feel would be helpful to "yield the right of way" to your partner or another family member. After each one, indicate how you are going to do it.

Exercise 3. If you were told that you have only one year to live, what plans would you make and what would you do during your final year of life? What would be your greatest priority? How would your life be different than the way you are presently living? Why?

Exercise 4. Which of the following kinds of decisions are most difficult for you to choose?

1. Disciplining of children
2. How and where to spend money
3. Relationship with in laws
4. Religious or church involvements
5. Planning vacations or how to spend leisure time

C. Identify Specific Values Related to Your Decision

Identify the values that are important to you and are related to the choice you must make. Your values are basically what your needs and interests are.

Exercise 1. Simply identify the things you want and

value in relation to this decision. Be honest. List at least five things. Write down the specifics and do not include general words such as "purity" or "happiness." Each of you should write down the values separately. In listing your values, simply answer, "What things are important to me in this decision and what do I want for myself?"

Exercise 2. Share and discuss with your partner the values you identified. Which values do you hold in common and which are different?

Now combine each list of values into one set. My wife and I identified and combined the following values related to our choice of job opportunities:

Job satisfaction
Satisfactory salary
Increased time together at home
Close home
Fellowship with Christians
Counseling opportunities
Employment for Joyce
Output experiences
Promotion opportunities
Input growth
Writing time
Aesthetic
Entertainment/Shopping

Exercise 3. Separately rank the combined set of values according to each one's personal attitudes and feelings. Be honest. Don't rank them in the way you think your partner expects.

Take turns sharing your hierarchy of values. Note the similarities and differences. Remember that you won't have the same order, so don't criticize or judge your partner.

D. Establish a Mutual Value System

Exercise 1: Separately assign a number from 0-100 to each item on the value hierarchy. This is to determine the relative importance or strength of each value. Carefully consider and compare the degree to which one value is greater than another. It is easier to use multiples of five. The values will differ in relative importance. When assigning numbers to each value answer the following questions:

(a) How important is this to me?

(b) How much more important is the value ranked #1 compared to the other values?

(c) If I could buy any of the values and possess it for many years how much would I be willing to pay for each? If I could spend only a limited amount of money, how much would I pay for each?

Discuss with each other the scored value systems. Try to increase your awareness of your partner's perceptions and understand his or her values more. Open yourself to new considerations. Note the values in which one person scored high and the other low. Take turns sharing why a particular value is high so that you may appreciate each other's beliefs and understand the need more accurately. Are there any values which were not included that need to be evaluated? Add to the list any values which were overlooked.

After both individuals separately assign a score to each value, write the value hierarchies for each person side by side. Then add the scores for each value item together to yield a combined scored value system.

As an example, my wife and I assigned the following numbers to each value on the hierarchy to show the relative impotance of the various factors for each of us:

COMBINED VALUE HIERARCHY

Value Item	Husband Scores	Wife Scores	Combined Value Scores
Job satisfaction	95	85	180
Satisfactory salary	90	80	170
Increased time together at home	80	95	175
Close home	50	90	140
Fellowship with Christians	70	75	145
Counseling opportunities	75	65	140
Employment for Joyce	65	70	135
Output experiences	60	55	115
Promotion opportunities	40	60	100
Input growth	55	50	105
Writing	45	40	85
Aesthetic	40	35	75
Entertainment/Shopping	20	30	50

The combined value weight for each item represents the new value structure based on the mutual needs of the couple. It is the couple's value system, no longer the husband's or the wife's but both. Thus the combined value structure is a unified system obtained from the needs and values of each spouse.

You may have noticed that for some values both the husband and wife have nearly identical scores. Other values show a significant discrepancy between the scores of husband and wife. For example, my wife and I had considerably different needs regarding the value of locating close home. However, the combined value system balances the differences.

Selection of Alternatives

The selection of alternatives involves a careful consideration of each option. To make intelligent rational decisions we must acquire factual information about the alternatives and evaluate the positives and negatives of them. We also need to determine the reward-cost factors to know if the decision will be worth our time and efforts.

A. *Consider Pertinent Information*

Exercise 1. Analyze what kind of information you need. Ask yourself the following questions and determine which is characteristic of your situation.

> Do I have the knowledge I need? If not, where can I get it?
>
> Do I know how to use the information I now have? If not, how can I learn how to use it?
>
> Do I know what information I need in order to decide? If not, how can I find out?

The information you do not have may be very important for the decision you make.

Exercise 2. Together write down the basic "facts" about each alternative. Identify clearly what is known about the options.

Exercise 3. Identify what expectations will be placed on you as a couple by selecting a given alternative. What are the responsibilities the option includes? Make a list of the duties and responsibilities you will have to perform.

Exercise 4. Discuss the options with friends and informed acquaintances. Consult specialists when appropriate in order to obtain relevant information.

B. *Evaluate the Alternatives*

Evaluate the alternatives according to your values. Estimate the degree to which each scored value could be satisfied by the alternative. Ask, "Does the alternative gratify or hinder the fulfillment of the value?" and "To what extent can the combined scored values system be satisfied by each alternative?"

a. At the top of a paper, write down one alternative. Then draw a line down the middle and make two columns. The left column is for writing the value items. The right column is for writing the combined value scores.

Example:

Alternative 1

Value	Combined Value Score
1.	
2.	
3.	

b. Estimate the extent that the alternative could satisfy each value—either completely, partially, or not at all.

(1) If the value score could be satisfied *completely*, then put the full score for that value.

(2) If the value could be satisfied *partially*, then use a fractional part (¼, ½, ¾) of the value score to estimate the degree of satisfaction.

(3) If the value could not be satisfied by the alternative, then place a zero instead of the value score.

c. For a value in which you cannot realistically estimate fulfillment, simply write in a zero.

As an example, my wife and I completed the task as shown on pages 65 and 66.

Alternative 1

Value	Scaled Weight Combined	
1. Job satisfaction	180	(definitely the type of work desired)
2. Satisfactory salary	125	(salary somewhat adequate but cost of living very high—¾ of 170)
3. Increased time together at home	0	(job demanded evening clinic work and occasional Saturdays)
4. Close home	0	(almost 400 miles away)
5. Fellowship with Christians	145	(Christian clinic active in dynamic fellowship)
6. Counseling opportunities	140	(job description included much counseling opportunities)
7. Employment for Joyce	135	(numerous opportunities for teaching or counseling jobs)
8. Output experiences	115	(excellent opportunity for leading retreats, seminars, etc.)
9. Promotion opportunities	50	(probably available but job description unclear (½ of 100)
10. Input growth	105	(excellent professional opportunities to attend conferences, etc.)
11. Writing	0	(limited or no time to write)
12. Aesthetic	0	(city undesirable location for us)
13. Entertainment/Shopping	50	(adequate—located in large city)
Total	995	

Alternative 2

Value	Scaled Weight Combined	
1. Job satisfaction	180	(definitely the type of work desired)
2. Satisfactory salary	170	(good salary; cost of living lower)
3. Increased time together at home	175	(home in the evening; flexible schedule; more vacation time)
4. Close home	140	(90 miles away)
5. Fellowship with Christians	0	(no knowledge of; couldn't estimate)
6. Counseling opportunities	140	(excellent—job description included it)
7. Employment for Joyce	70	(probability about half—but not highly encouraging (½ of 135)
8. Output experiences	85	(adequate, but not as great—¾ of 115)
9. Promotion opportunities	100	(sufficient—specifics included in job description)
10. Input growth	0	(no evidence of professional input opportunities at this time)
11. Writing	85	(adequate time to write)
12. Aesthetic	75	(beautiful scenic mountains)
13. Entertainment/Shopping	0	(definitely insufficient)
Total	1220	

Although both opportunities offered many positive aspects, the second alternative had the greatest potential of meeting our collective needs. The third option which was not discussed yielded a score of less than 400 and was discarded.

C. Analyze the Risk and Reward Cost Factors

Choosing is risk-taking. We cannot predict the outcomes specifically and certainly can't control the circumstances. Every decision we make bears an element of risk. Each of us has an internal level which dictates the amount of risk we are able and willing to take. The readiness to select an alternative is related to our understanding of the sacrifices we will have to make and a belief that we can succeed in the decision. Since succeeding is one of our highest values, we make decisions that we believe have a strong probability of success and avoid other alternatives.

Exercise 1. Discuss the advantages and disadvantages of each option. What does each option have to offer you? Write down the sacrifices you may have to make for each alternative or what you may have to give up. Discuss together if the gains are greater than the sacrifices.

Exercise 2. Consider what positive attributes you possess that will be helpful to you in fulfilling the responsibilities of each option. Complete these sentences in as many ways as possible:

"What I have to offer is" . . .
"My strong points are" . . .

Exercise 3. After writing the list of duties/responsibilities of a given option, put a "yes" or "no" behind each one indicating whether or not you believe you can fulfill it satisfactorily. Be honest and try to avoid responding with, "I don't know." You may find it helpful to seek the opinion of trusted friends to help you evaluate your strengths and weaknesses realistically.

Exercise 4. Consider your risk-taking tendencies. Are you likely to be very cautious or more adventurous and chance-taking? After you and your partner each complete the risk scale, discuss your differences and the implications. Avoid using 5.

Rating

1	2	3	4	5	6	7	8	9	10
Safe									**Risky**

Discuss at least two previous decisions you made recently; share how risky you were. What effect did that have on your partner?

Commitment to the Decision

Sometimes we have difficulty acting on a decision, even when we are reasonably certain which option to choose. This may be related to internal factors or external barriers. Making a successful decision involves assessing our priorities and time commitments as well as overcoming the barriers that hinder our choices. Leona Tyler wrote, "A decision is good if the person who makes it is completely willing to take its consequences." The willingness to accept responsibility for a personal decision is the key to successful living. Growth is possible only if we own the choices we make, and accept the consequences realistically.

A Decision-Making Plan for Couples

A. Consider Priorities and Time

Exercise 1. Do you have the time available that is required to fulfill the decision? Are you willing to invest the time in order to perform the responsibilities to your satisfaction?

A certain alternative may be very attractive, but if you can't make the time available for it, you will only be frustrated and discouraged. The Scriptures admonish us to make the best use of our time, to think and act carefully, and to evaluate our time commitments.

> So be careful how you act; these are difficult days. Don't be fools; be wise: make the most of every opportunity you have for doing good. Ephesians 5:15, 16, *Living Bible*.

Exercise 2. What priority shifting will you have to do in order to make the decision? What might have to be dropped to carry out the demands of your choice? Reflect upon your priorities. A good indicator of your true priorities is the amount of time spent each week in a given activity. You may say that reading is top priority but spend 10-15 hours a week watching television and five hours reading. To get in touch with your energy commitments, try recording the frequency or time involved in your daily activities. Those activities with the greatest frequency and time are the ones that will most likely block you from attaining your goals and fulfilling your desired responsibilities.

Exercise 3. What amount of energy must you commit to make the choice and fulfill its obligations? Are you in a flexible enough position to act or is it going to require too much energy investment? You can only be involved to the point of your physical, emotional, and psychological limits. Many people weary themselves and others by making commitments which require more energy than they are able to give.

B. Accept and Act on the Choice

Exercise 1. Draw a line down the middle of a piece of paper. On the left side, write down the real or perceived barriers (both within and outside yourself) which are keeping you from acting. On the right side, list steps you could take to remove each barrier.

Exercise 2. Are you willing to accept the consequences of the choice even if the outcomes are different than expected? Try to make a small and simple vow to one another that you will help each other adjust and encourage each other in the decision.

Exercise 3. Everyone needs support, especially after making a difficult decision. How can you support your partner in the choice? List at least three specific things you can do that will help your partner adjust to or fulfill the responsibilities of the decision.

Exercise 4. How can you avoid condemning yourself if the outcomes seem undesirable? Discuss Phillippians 3:14, 15 and 1 Thessalonians 5:16-18.

Exercise 5. If you had the opportunity to choose again, what option would you select? Why? Is there anything you would do differently in making the decision?

Spiritual Resources for Making Decisions

There is an admitted tendency in all of us to seek the consolation of God rather than the God of consolations.

John Powell in
He Touched Me

CHAPTER 5

Spiritual Resources For Making Decisions

The Scriptures are provided as our guide to truth. They cut into our daily existence with piercing forcefulness. The Scriptures both comfort and confront us; they fill us with hope and sobriety. They are given to us in wisdom so that we may know the Author of Wisdom. They contain basic life principles to guide us and provide essential knowledge regarding the decision-making process.

Principle 1. A disciplined mind and realistic thinking are essential ingredients in making decisions.

In 2 Timothy 1:7 the Scriptures reveal that "God has

given to us a spirit of *sound mind.*" The Greek word (*sophronismos*) implies self-discipline, prudence, and an attitude of careful consideration which produces good judgment. This attitude of thoughtful self-control in decision-making is congruent with the Spirit of God. It is both our privilege and responsibility to use our minds reasonably. We do not need to be fearful or anxious when making decisions, but can use the minds God gave us to consider each alternative with clarity.

Our responsibility to God and ourselves is to execute sound judgment in making decisions. This involves a careful process of considering the positives and negatives of each alternative and evaluating them in light of God's revealed Word.

The Apostle Paul spoke of thinking soberly (*sophroneo*) in Romans 12:3. In this passage, he contrasted having an attitude of distorted and conceited thinking with a sensible, realistic attitude. The believer is to be moderate and exercise sober judgment with the recognition that God has given to him a measure of faith. Realistic judgment develops from a proper understanding of self. This requires an honest assessment of personal motives, strengths, and weaknesses. Understanding our identity and accepting who we are constitute the basis for being able to make wise decisions. But knowing oneself requires honest, disciplined thinking. I am reminded of the words of George Eliot,

> Falsehood is so easy, truth so difficult! Examine your words well and you will find that even when you have no motive to be false it is very hard to say that exact truth, even about your own immediate feelings—much harder than to say something fine about them which is not the exact truth.

To examine our words conscientiously and search our motives honestly is the kernel of being sober in thought. Apostle Peter utilized a similar concept when writing to Jewish Christians. In 1 Peter 1:13 we read, "Gird up your minds, be sober, set your hope fully upon the grace that is coming to you at the revelation of Jesus Christ." The Greek word for mind is *dianoia,* which means a thinking through process, meditation, and reflecting. The verse implies that we gain understanding and knowledge in making moral decisions through meditation upon God's Word and serious reflection upon our identity and circumstances. Peter used the phrase "gird up" which metaphorically means to get ready and be mentally alert for action. Perhaps the modern athletic concept of "getting psyched up" is applicable. When was the last time you got psyched up about making an important decision? How do you mentally prepare yourself so you are spiritually and emotionally alert to the possibilities?

Decision-making is a challenging task which requires both sobriety and excitement. The latter part of the verse in 1 Peter uniquely connects the revelation of Jesus Christ with the process of girding our minds. As we meditate and reflect, we become open to receive God's revelation through Christ. God promises that He will grant us understanding to make decisions. 1 John 5:20 says, "And we know that the Son of God has come and has given us understanding." James 1:5 adds, "If you want to know what God wants you to do, ask him, and he will gladly tell you, for he is always ready to give a bountiful supply of wisdom to all who ask him; he will not resent it" (*Living Bible*).

Principle 2. We are instructed to actively seek God's will in decision-making.

Ephesians 5:17 says, "Don't act thoughtlessly, but try to find out and do whatever the Lord wants you to" (*Living Bible*). Also in Ephesians 5:10 we read, "And try to learn what is pleasing to the Lord."

These verses indicate that knowing God's will is a learning process. It is an active and careful consideration of who God is and who man is. We can't just passively sit and hope for some lightning flash or handwriting on the wall to reveal to us the right choice. We are instructed by God's Word to apply our capacities and commit our energies to search for the will of the Lord. We are fools if we do not seek to learn His will and unwise if we do not carefully evaluate our manner of living.

Paul Little points out that many Christians view God's will as a possession, something you have or don't have. They ask, "Have you discovered God's will for your life?"—as though God's will is a special blueprint handed to us. He suggests that this is a misconception since God's will is really a process. The Christian life is a step-by-step experience, not a canned format![1] Someone has commented that the only way to see far ahead in the will of God is to go ahead just as far as you can see.

There is no prescribed formula for knowing God's will. However, God's will has two obvious aspects—that which has been revealed clearly in His Word and the part in which God has not set down specific guidelines. Paul Little states, further:

> By recognizing the two aspects of God's will—that which is already revealed in His Word, and those areas about which He is not specific—you get away from the static concept of the blueprint. The will of God is not a package let down from heaven on a string.
>
> It is far more like a scroll that unrolls every day. God has a

will for you and me today, tomorrow, and the next day and the day after that. Everyone of us continues to seek the will of God throughout the whole of our lives. . . . Because of this, our call is not basically to follow a plan, a blueprint, a place, or a work, but our call is basically to follow the Lord Jesus Christ.[2]

We cannot know God's will apart from His Word; they are inseparable. C. S. Lewis commented that the Bible is like an accurate and detailed map that leads us to God. Without the map of Scriptures, our knowledge of God and His will is very limited. The Scriptures are filled with hundreds of specific instructions, examples, and guidelines essential for making decisions congruent with God's will. R. B. Thieme uses an enlightening illustration from algebra:

> "X" equals the unknown factor, but X cannot be determined without known factors around it. While X is unknown, as soon as we place known factors around it, we can determine what X is. For example, if 2X = 10, what is X? Answer: X = 5. The reason we know that X equals five is because we have known factors in the picture. Known factors determine the meaning of X.[3]

He points out that the known factors of divine guidance are reported in Scripture. With the known factors, we can determine the unknown and thus make decisions in accord with God's will.

Sometimes we expect God to encounter us with blind-

---

1. Paul Little, *Affirming the Will of God* (Downers Grove, Ill.: Inter-Varsity Press, 1971).
2. *Ibid.*, pp. 56, 57.
3. R. B. Thieme, *Divine Guidance* (Houston, Tex.: Berachah Tapes and Publications, 1966), p. 3.

ing light as He did the Apostle Paul. With a touch of vanity, we anticipate that God will treat us with special attention and favor us with some outstanding revelation. We may even become insulted when we pray for God to reveal His will and several weeks later we are still faced with the same decision. The thought of actively seeking God's will seems undesirable. But God has already revealed His will in the Scriptures, and through consistent prayer and honest study, we can discover His revealed truth. Our greatest growth comes in the process of seeking God's truth and learning what is acceptable to God.

Let us not be lazy Christians regarding this truth. May God help us to search the Scriptures daily as did the Beroeans (Acts 17:11).

I am amazed at the words of Jesus regarding His relationship to the Father. Read carefully John 5:19, 20, 30; John 6:38-40; John 7:16-18; John 8:28, 29; and Hebrews 10:5-10. Note several basic concepts that were true for Jesus. Since He is our Example, these principles become truth for us also (1 Peter 1:21).

1. *Jesus did nothing on His own accord, or in His own strength.* The Son could do nothing through His own power. The actions of His life were an expression of the power of the Holy Spirit in Him by the authority of the Father. *Total dependence* upon God was His experience. Perfect unity and intimacy existed between Jesus and God. Jesus depended upon God—and we as God's children must also totally depend upon the Father. We cannot make right decisions without depending upon God for His revelation and the strength to carry out the choices.

In the second book of *The Chronicles of Narnia,* C. S.

Lewis beautifully illustrates God's attitude toward our dependency upon the Creator. The God-figure is a magnificent and glorious lion named Aslan. Aslan asked a youthful prince if the man felt sufficient to take up the Kingdom of Narnia. The man replied in honest humility that he was only a boy and did not have the wisdom or strength to be king. Aslan compassionately responded,

> If you had felt yourself sufficient, it would have been a proof that you were not. Therefore, under us and under the High King, you shall be King of Narnia.[4]

In honesty and weakness we find our strength. God knows that we must depend fully upon Him for the power to live joyfully and meaningfully. The more we accept our dependency, the more free and fulfilled life becomes.

2. *God revealed to the Son all that was to be done and the Father gave Jesus the power to do it.* How often we fret needlessly over decisions. Jesus knew the Father's will through complete reliance on God, and God faithfully made known to Jesus His Will. Also God empowered Christ with the ability to exercise truth through the Holy Spirit. Jesus was filled with the Spirit and lived in union with God (Matthew 4:4). God will likewise make known to us all that is to be done. Philippians 2:13 assures us that God is at work in us helping us to experience His will and empowering us to live as we should.

3. *Jesus actively sought to do the will of the Father.*

4. C. S. Lewis, *The Chronicles of Narnia*, Book 2 (New York: Macmillan, 1970), p. 200.

He came to earth to exercise God's will and renounce His own will. His purpose in living was to glorify the Father through loving obedience. Christ emptied Himself of natural desires and relinquished His rights to the Father. He humbled Himself and became obedient unto death (Philippians 2:5-11). Jesus yielded to the will of God. Therefore, God highly exalted Him. Likewise, we experience the glory of God when we yield to His will and regularly pray, "Not my will, but Thine be done." Paul instructs us to set our "affections on things above, not on things on the earth." (Colossians 3:2). This involves an attitude which values God's truth more than man's pleasure, a process of choosing loving obedience to God instead of acting on our passions. (See Romans 6:12, 13.)

God has given to us a tremendous promise that He will supply all our needs. Philippians 4:19 says, "My God will supply every need of yours according to his riches in glory in Christ Jesus." In Matthew 6, Jesus reminds us that we need not be anxious about our lives for our loving heavenly Father knows all of our needs. But we are to seek first His kingdom and all these things shall be given to us. Proverbs 3:5, 6 assures us that when we trust in the Lord and not upon our limited understanding, God will direct our paths.

In deciding whether or not to enter the ministry, Alan Redpath systematically sought the will of God. He reported that he made a list of the arguments in favor of staying in business. Every day he conscientiously prayed that God would show him specific verses that would counter each argument if God wanted him to leave the business and enter the ministry. He discovered that God daily spoke to him through the Scriptures and by the end of a year each argument had been annihilated with Scripture verses. He states: "It took over a year, but I was not in a hurry. I was willing to wait; I wanted it to be in God's time. Too much was at stake to dash into the thing. I wanted to intelligently find the will of God."[5]

Principle 3. The Christian is instructed to make decisions conformable to God and not in agreement with worldly opinions.

Romans 12:2 contains an important perspective for decision-making. "Do not be conformed to this world but be transformed by the renewal of your mind, that you may prove what is the will of God, what is good and acceptable and perfect."

"Do not be conformed to this world." The believer is not to align his goals with those of the world. Conformity (*suschematizo*) means to be fashioned outwardly or shaped like another thing. If the Christian's aspirations and goals are fashioned according to the world, then his decisions will be contrary to God's purpose and he will experience diverse negative consequences.

Fred was a believer who failed to follow this principle. He set his ambitions upon accumulating wealth and recognition. To be highly esteemed as a prestigious businessman in his community became more important than loving God. He made several important decisions that were in agreement with his business cronies but contrary to Scripture. These included cheating on his income tax, refusing to tithe, and buying unnecessary leisure items which he seldom used in order to impress the neighbors.

One night at an office party, Fred was drinking

5. Alan Redpath, *Getting to Know the Will of God* (Downers Grove, Ill.: Inter-Varsity Press).

heavily. His friends dared him to try "making it" with his secretary. Deep inside, he knew his values were opposed to extramarital sex. However, he felt the pressure to conform and did not want to appear weak or "holier than thou." Considering his alcoholic intake, his moral inhibitions were lessened and after much cajoling from his friends he complied. Had Fred previously developed a pattern of conforming to the Scriptures instead of worldly goals, he probably would have had the courage to say "no". But he rationalized that night, saying it really didn't matter and that this was a once in a lifetime experience. The incident proved disastrous and was the beginning of a severe breakdown with his wife and a miserable marriage.

Value clarification is an important avenue for setting goals which are uniquely different from the world. The Christian's values are essentially different from the non-Christian. Values are a primary motivating force in one's life. Any decision which is contrary to biblical values will most certainly result in dissonance and inner misery for the Christian.

The Apostle Peter comments on the same concept. He admonishes believers to be obedient to God and not to pattern their lives according to their former state of ignorance before salvation (1 Peter 1:14-16). Christians are called to be holy, and God makes the believer holy in Christ. Therefore, if we choose to conform to the world or align our wills with the natural desires, we forfeit the beautiful experience of allowing God to make us like Christ. Our choice to live for personal pleasure always produces a corruption in our identity and results in confusion, interpersonal alienation, and lack of fulfillment. An individual only discovers real fulfillment through allowing God to mold him to become like Christ. This involves an active decision to say "no" to the world and "yes" to Christ.

Moses, the lawgiver, demonstrated this attitude. The Scriptures say,

> By faith Moses, when he was grown up, refused to be called the son of Pharaoh's daughter, choosing rather to share ill-treatment with the people of God than to enjoy the fleeting pleasures of sin. Hebrews 11:24, 25.

Moses refused to conform to the immense pressure of accepting the Egyptian rulership. He could have had anything he wanted and his resources for pleasure were unlimited. He could have been the rightful heir to the throne of Egypt which was the wealthiest and most powerful nation in the world at that time. What a fantastic chance to say "yes" to his Egyptian heritage and comply with the Pharaoh's wishes. But he chose obedience to God and became a slave.

These passages clearly instruct believers to refrain from seeking the approval and confirmation of unbelievers. As the psalmist succinctly wrote, "Blessed is the man who walks not in the counsel of the wicked" (Psalm 1:1). The Christian is not to seek affirmation on decisions from nonbelievers. What the world considers important is very different from the Christian perspective. If the believer tries to please the world by making decisions that conform to its expectations, only confusion and turmoil result. God reveals in 1 Corinthians 1 and 2 that His wisdom is foolishness to the world. The unspiritual man cannot know the things of God. The unbeliever is not in a position to discern spiritual truth, for such truth is revealed by the Spirit of God. The unbeliever is not concerned with doing the will of God and his decisions are based on gratification of self. Seeking the approval and aligning your decisions with what nonbelievers expect or advise is definitely inappropriate for Christians.

This does not mean that we should avoid seeking advice from expert consultants. Valuable information and insight can be gained by listening to the counsel of professionals or knowledgeable people in various disciplines. The more significant information we obtain the better we are able to assess needs and consider alternatives wisely. However, in the decision-making process, our choices must be based upon the values clarified by scriptural principles rather than the value structure of nonbelievers.

"*But be transformed by the renewal of your mind.*"

Transformation is a process somewhat like metamorphosis. The insect larva which spins a cocoon undergoes an intricate process of changing form. During the incubation and waiting period, God's miraculous forces are at work creating a new and glorious form. The larva is transformed from a humble wormlike creature to a marvelous butterfly that is *free* to enjoy the earth and return glory to God. So it is with us. God transforms us and makes us new creatures. But let us carefully observe this unique truth.

a. Transformation or metamorphosis is a process, a gradual ongoing development toward wholeness or perfection. It does not occur suddenly. We do not experience wholeness and maturity instantaneously but rather through a growth process in which God's miracle of grace is actualized in our lives. Transformation is not hopping from one "peak experience" to another, nor does it consist of "spiritual highs." Transformation is the process of living in which God makes us like Christ and conforms us to the image of His Son (Romans 8:29). Paul beautifully wrote, "We all, with unveiled face, beholding the glory of the Lord, are being changed into his likeness from one degree of glory to another; for this comes from the Lord who is the Spirit" (2 Corinthians 3:18). Being changed *by degrees* as we look into the revealed glory of God and the resurrected Christ! There are no shortcuts to being made whole or becoming sanctified. The metamorphosis is God's miracle of love in the fullness of time.

b. The larva enters a cocoon in a resting stage and waits for the creative miracle. And so it should be with us as we wait upon God, willing to let Him make us whole in His way and in His time. Too often we are impatient. We want to be perfect now! We want to have everything in God's will for us immediately. We don't want to *wait* and simply *rest* in God's promises. But the transformation process is related to our willingness to wait with patience and trust God to fulfill His will in us. Unlike the larva that rests, we struggle to be "good Christians" and often feel discouragement. We try to transform ourselves through our own efforts and good deeds and forget that metamorphosis is God's miracle—not ours. We need to remind ourselves constantly that God is at work in us to do His will through us (Hebrews 13:20, 21).

Paul admonishes us to wait with patience for the things we hope for. He adds that the Holy Spirit helps us in our weakness during the process of growth and makes intercession for us in accordance with God's will (Romans 8:25-27.) God Himself works in us to do His will and the Holy Spirit prays for us while God transforms us. What a privilege it is to wait with patience and receive God's promises!

c. Waiting is not a passive, nonchalant state. Rather it is an active process of "renewing our minds." Transformation occurs as we yield to the power of Christ in us. Renewal is the process of adjusting one's moral vision and thinking God's thoughts. It is the process of willingly submitting to God, the response of the believer in allowing the Holy Spirit to direct and guide him. The wild stallion does not lose its power and dignity when it is tamed. Rather the horse becomes more admirable because its strength and beauty are willingly submitted to the master's touch. Now its energy is directed through the wisdom and love of the master. So it is with the believer.

Renewal of the mind involves a desire to receive God's promises, the dedicated search for truth in the Scriptures, and an ongoing commitment to the revealed truth. The process of renewal is the work of the Holy Spirit in response to our willingness to be changed. We must be teachable in order to learn. The psalmist proclaimed, "The sacrifice acceptable to God is a broken spirit; a broken and contrite heart, Oh God, thou wilt not despise" (Psalm 51:17). Our desire must be to love God with our heart, soul and mind, and to love our neighbor (Matthew 22:37).

"*That you may prove what is the will of God, what is good and acceptable and perfect.*"

Discovering God's will comes through renewal of the mind. We verify that our decision is in agreement with God through this process. We can test or actualize our decision with confidence. Everyone wants to make the best decisions, to do the right thing. The Christian has the capacity through the working of the Holy Spirit to choose what is intrinsically good and acceptable to God.

The decision that is acceptable to God is the most rewarding and fulfilling experience. As we consciously seek God's will and seriously explore ourselves, the right decisions will be made. God makes Himself known and we have the confidence by faith that we are doing what is right.

Principle 4. Ask in prayer and it shall be given us. Wait with patience.

How beautiful the words of Jesus in Matthew 7, "Ask, and it will be given you; seek, and you will find; knock, and it will be opened to you" (Matthew 7:7). There are no loopholes in this passage. God doesn't play games with us. The simple truth is that if we seek and ask, we shall receive from the Father, the Giver of all good gifts.

Prayer is essential for receiving. Honest prayer with a contrite heart is the key to understanding what the will of God is. Abraham Lincoln said,

> I have been driven many times to my knees by the overwhelming conviction that I had nowhere else to go. My own wisdom, and that of all about me, seemed insufficient for the day.

The Scriptures are filled with God's promise that if we ask anything in the name of Jesus according to the will of the Father, it will be given to us. Read the following representative passages and let the Holy Spirit confirm these promises: John 14:12-14; John 15:7, 8; John 16:23, 24; and Matthew 6:25-34. These are the words of Christ Himself to us. No greater veracity can be found than in the words of Christ our Lord. Likewise, consider God's promises as disclosed by other writers; Philippians 4:6, 7; 1 John 5:14, 15; James 5:14-18; Hebrews 4:14-16; and Hebrews 10:19-25.

God wants us to know and do His will. The Spirit wants to control and guide our lives in *all* truth. When we sincerely seek His will, God makes known in our hearts His truth. Whoever, whenever, whatever, wherever, anything, all, everything—are the all-inclusive words that God gives to us in His promises.

Oh, but you say, "I have prayed and nothing happens! I talked to God several months ago about this situation but God hasn't answered me yet. Why doesn't He tell me something concrete? If God hears prayer, then what's He doing taking all this time to answer?" Impatience wells up. You become angry and feel mistreated. You have difficulty accepting God's timing and you lose hope. You may even sadly conclude that you must not be spiritual enough or that God's promises are only for the special saints.

How easy it is to grow weary with the growth process of God's timing. We want answers now! We expect God to jump into the circumstances and solve the problem with a flair of majesty. Because God doesn't respond the way we desire, we erroneously conclude that His promises are not for us. How sad! We miss so much blessing by assuming that we have to be something special or be good enough to earn God's promises. His promises are true for every believer. They are our possession and privilege. We can't earn them and we certainly will never deserve those blessings. No Christian is righteous enough to receive from God those blessings. God forbid! No, God gives them to us by His grace—to every Christian—because He has redeemed us and made us His sons. His promises are experienced simply by accepting them and believing that His word is truth.

Many of us tire of praying. We lack the perseverance

of seeking God's will. In a dilemma we get frustrated at what seems to be the silence of God and give up. We ignore the verses such as Ephesians 6:18; 1 Thessalonians 5:17, 18; and Luke 18:1. Praying, like growth, is a process. It involves an attitude of honestly seeking God's will and willingly accepting God's Word. Effective praying is not a spasmodic activity. Prayer requires mental alertness and energy commitment. The writer of Hebrews says that Jesus worked hard at prayer, offering supplications with loud cries and tears. True intercession is costly. Prayer is a process of saying regularly to God what Jesus said daily, "Not my will, but Thine be done."

Asking for a certain request is only a small portion of prayer. The ongoing prayer of our heart must be to love God and become obedient to His revealed truth.

Prayer requires patience. We hope for the things we ask, even though we don't see them or know how we will receive them. But the waiting process is so hard. In our fast technical society, we are not acquainted with waiting. Meditation and silence is rarely a part of our living. We are in a hurry. But we cannot hurry the growth processes, nor can we receive truth when we don't take the time to wait.

The prophet speaks deeply to our impatience in chapter 40 of Isaiah. How often we have cried out words like these: "My way is hid from the Lord and my right is disegarded by my God." But God answers with a beautiful voice that echoes throughout the heavens into our hearts: "Have you not known? Have you not heard? The Lord is the everlasting God, the Creator of the ends of the earth. He does not faint or grow weary, his understanding is unsearchable. He gives power to the faint, and to him who has no might he increases strength"

(Isaiah 40:28, 29). Yes, even strong men and faithful saints become weary and faint. But how rich is God's promise to us if we are willing to *wait* upon the Lord: "They who wait for the Lord shall renew their strength, they shall mount up with wings like eagles, they shall run and not be weary, they shall walk and not faint" (Isaiah 40:31).

How can we find the strength and patience to wait? "I hurt now and I want the pain removed immediately," we may say. "I have very little time to make this decision and I need answers soon." God has provided a comforting promise for the waiting periods. In Romans 8:24-29, we find the answer. While we hope and wait, the Holy Spirit helps us in our weakness. God Himself strengthens us. His Spirit makes intercession for us according to the will of God. Yes, even when we don't know how to pray, or are too frustrated to form words upon our lips, the Holy Spirit prays for us. He serves as our advocate to the Father in our many moments of weakness. How beautiful that God so understands our infirmities and so loves us that He provides His Spirit to pray with and for us (1 Corinthians 2:10-16). Jesus empathizes with us in our weaknesses. He understands our needs and experiences them with us. Therefore, we can come with confidence to God, even when we don't know how to pray, since the Spirit understands our infirmities and makes intercession for us.

It is no marvel then that "All things work together for good to them that love God, to them who are the called according to his purpose." (Romans 8:28). But we must realize that His purpose is to make us like Christ and that is a lifetime growth process.

Quoting again from *The Chronicles of Narnia,* C. S.

Lewis describes the end product of this growth process through the characters' interaction with the God-figure, Aslan the lion. Lucy, one of the little girls in the story, comes face-to-face with Aslan after a time lapse of several years.

> She gazed up into the large wise face.
> "Welcome, child," he said.
> "Aslan," said Lucy, "you're bigger."
> "That is because you are older, little one," answered he. "Not because you are?"
> "I am not. But every year you grow, you will find me bigger."[6]

God is always bigger than our decisions, and the more we know God the greater he seems.

Sometimes we are like the child who plants a seed and is so anxious for it to grow, that he digs it up to see how it's doing. We are too concerned about getting the end product instead of allowing the maturing process to develop. The tree does not bear fruit until several years of rootedness and acquiring strength.

Sometimes we feel so confused that we have little understanding of what to pray. I believe in these moments we experience the greatest growth by honestly expressing these feelings aloud to God and simply thanking Him that He understands. As we ask God to teach us to pray, the Holy Spirit will help us to pray. Perhaps the first request to be uttered from our lips should be, "Lord . . . teach me to do thy will" (Psalm 143:9, 10). In the same breath, we can say with the psalmist, "Search me, O God, and know my heart! Try me and know my

6. *Op. cit., Prince Caspian,* p. 136.

thoughts! And see if there be any wicked way in me, and lead me in the way everlasting" (Psalm 139:23, 24). To be taught and searched by God requires time. We must sit before the Lord in silence and allow His Spirit to make known His ways. God desires to reveal Himself to every person, but we must be willing to be still and listen "Be still, and know that I am God" (Psalm 46:10).

Sometimes our prayers are meaningless because of our anxiety. Jo Kimmel emphasizes that relaxation is essential for effective prayer. Relaxation allows tension to be released and a calm spirit to flow in us. She points out that perhaps we do not hear God's communication to us because we are so anxious and tight about our state of affairs. To be taught is to listen. In order to listen carefully, we must be relaxed and at ease. "It may be we who need changing," she reminds us. "So always ask for more light into your own motives and ask God to align them with His will."[7] She suggests that we must ask God to reveal to us how to change ourselves instead of thinking only that the other person must change. Let God show us our responsibility.

"Every promise of God finds its affirmative in him, and through him can be said the final Amen, to the glory of God" (2 Corinthians 1:20, *Phillips*). As you meditate on God's promises, recognize the entirety and all inclusiveness of them. As you carefully read them, open yourself to receiving blessings from God.

> Prayer is not a substitute for the hard work of thinking about the alternatives which face us. Some people erro-

7. Jo Kimmel, *Steps to Prayer Power* (Nashville, Tenn.: Abingdon Press, 1976), pp. 54, 55.

> neously contrast prayer and work or prayer and thought, but these are not opposites. These people would become childish (not childlike) in their attempt to let God take over the responsibility for their lives. . . . Jesus regarded prayer as the accompaniment of effort and an alternative to despairing acquiescence and inertia. Prayer is work. Throughout the New Testament, the opposite of praying about a thing is to do nothing, and the opposite of working for a cause is to stop praying.[8]

Principle 5. On certain occasions, fasting may be necessary to discern the best decision.

The purpose of fasting is always to draw persons into a deeper union with God. Fasting is a process of setting aside physical gratification in order to experience a more intimate relationship with the loving Father. It is designed to quicken the spiritual faculties of the believer so that God may work more freely.

In fasting, the individual willingly refuses to partake of physical food from one day to several days or weeks. The length of fasting is unique to each occasion based upon the intensity of personal needs and urgency to receive God's filling.

Fasting develops out of stressful circumstances in which the individual feels compelled to seek truth and is overwhelmed with a desire to receive understanding from God. The source of fasting can be varied, but is usually accompanied with an emotional intensity related to personal needs. The Scriptures describe several distinct occasions for fasting:

— For deliverance from enemies or disaster (2 Chronicles 20; 1 Samuel 7; Acts 27).

---

8. Roy W. Fairchild, *Christians in Families* (Atlanta, Ga.: John Knox, 1964), pp. 192, 193.

— In face of national calamity (Nehemiah 1, 2; Esther 4).
— For divine guidance in decision-making (Acts 13:1-4; Acts 14:21-23).
— For wisdom and understanding (Daniel 9; Ezra 8).
— For repentance, salvation, or regret over sins (Exodus 32—34; Jonah 3; 1 Samuel 7; 1 Kings 21:20-29; Joel 2:12-15).
— In face of severe temptation (Matthew 4: Luke 4).
— In preparation for ministry (Acts 9:1-9; 1 Kings 19; Exodus 24:15-18; Luke 4).
— For sorrow and mourning (2 Samuel).

Jesus taught that some situations cannot be overcome without fasting and prayer (Matthew 17:14-21). In that passage the casting out of demons required an intimate faith in God which is attainable only through fasting and prayer. Jesus clarified that the disciples' lack of faith prohibited them from casting out the demon.

The Master Teacher provided a word of caution pertaining to fasting. In Matthew 6:16-18, Jesus established that fasting was a personal communion between God and the believer to be done in secret without show. Annointing the head and washing the face symbolize the necessity of initiating a fast with confession and cleansing so that the Holy Spirit may fill the believer completely. Fasting should never be for recognition from others or selfish ambition which leads to spiritual pride. Fasting from selfish motives is unacceptable to God. (See Isaiah 58 and Jeremiah 14:10-12.)

It is imperative to honestly seek our motives and ask God to search our hearts when we fast. Allow God to reveal any wickedness, any slight tinge of pride, or any selfish ambition. The objective of fasting is to bring us into willing submission to God. Fasting and prayer provide the way to intimate communion with the Creator so that the purposes of Christ will take absolute first place in our lives. Christ preeminent means deliverance from all enemies—the world, flesh, and Satan. As Gordon Lindsey has noted, fasting and prayer are the key to the impossible. But the aim in fasting is to willingly crucify anything that comes between oneself and the Holy Spirit.[9]

Fasting is wrestling with our souls in which we seek to eliminate anything that interfers with total submission to God. We must deny our rights and desires so that no selfish influence can hinder God's power working freely in us. Fasting and prayer are the avenues to being made whole so that God's pure channel of love and wisdom and power may flow through us into others. In trying situations or when facing difficult decisions, you may need to accompany your prayers with fasting. It may be the conscientious self-sacrificing attitude that God desires of you in certain dilemmas before He makes known His will to you on a specific matter.

9. Gordon Lindsey, *Fasting and Prayer: The Key to the Impossible,* 1971.

Choice, an Exercise of Faith

Faith . . . is the confident assurance that something we want is going to happen. It is the certainty that what we hope for is waiting for us, even though we cannot see it up ahead.

Hebrews 11:1,
Living Bible

CHAPTER 6

Choice, an Exercise of Faith

Every decision is ultimately made by faith. Each choice is exercised on the basis of partial knowledge. No one possesses complete knowledge of self or all the factors involved to be able to predict outcomes. Decisions are an exercise of the will expressed through faith in the knowledge one has acquired. Choosing is a step of faith. The key question is, "In what does one place his trust and have faith?" This question leads into the whole area of value clarification and what one personally believes.

The choice one makes is an act of faith according to the values which one holds. This is the dividing line between a person who espouses Christian truth and one who does not. For the Christian, the choice is an act of faith in God and a trust that God is true and will fulfill His promises. For the unbeliever, the choice is an act of faith in oneself and trust in his own abilities. The non-Christian chooses on the basis of self-sufficiency, faith in his own human potentialities. The Christian chooses on the basis of God's sufficiency, faith in God's life-giving power.

For the Christian, the Scriptures are the primary reference point in decision-making. The essential question is, "Does the choice seem congruent with the will of God? What decision is in line with God's will?" For the nonbeliever, the desire to know and obey God's will is irrelevant. His decisions are ultimately based upon what will bring the most satisfaction to himself. The believer has the assurance of numerous promises from God. The nonbeliever does not perceive the supernatural as important in his life.

It is our responsibility to search ourselves and the Scriptures in clarifying values and evaluating alternatives. It is our responsibility to ascertain what the will of God is and then step out in faith. The Christian's decision-making responsibility is to choose by faith in accordance with revealed truth and let the rest up to God. God never takes us out on a limb and cuts the limb off behind us. However, He does let us onto the limb. God is faithful. We can count on that. He desires that we trust Him, and that's impossible if we refuse to step out and stop protecting ourselves.

Sometimes decision-making is tough because two alternatives look attractive and both are in agreement with scriptural principles. We may pray for wisdom and direction, but receive no specific guidance from God on which choice to select. We wonder which is the right decision. The whole area seems gray and one option appears as valid as the other. Yet we must choose. In decisions like that, you simply choose one and trust that God will be with you in the choice.

A. W. Tozer observed,

> Except for those things that are specifically commanded or forbidden in the Scriptures, it is God's will that we be free to exercise our own intelligent choice. In almost everything that touches our everyday life on earth, God is pleased when we're pleased. He wills that we be as free as birds to soar and sing our Maker's praise without anxiety. God's choice for us may not be only one but rather any one of a score of possible choices. The man or woman who is wholly and joyously surrendered to Christ can't make a wrong choice—any choice will be the right one.[1]

Tozer also uses the analogy that if God gives a man a compass He expects the man to use the compass wisely, with discretion, and not plead with God to show him the way to go. The action is our choice and it is a step of faith in God and His promises.

We do not need to fret by asking ourselves, "Is this the right decision?" when we have searched the Scriptures and are yielded to God. Any number of choices we initiate can be right. God is not likely to show us a blueprint, since the Christian life is a step by step, day by day walk with Christ (Proverbs 3:5, 6).

We say we are afraid of failing, that we can't make it. Jesus responds to that as He did to the disciples, "O thou

---

1. A. W. Tozer, "Four Ways to Find God's Will," *His* Magazine, May 1969.

of little faith." If we apply the principles of Scripture and trust God, we *can't fail!* God is committed to His children and by virtue of His nature, He cannot permit us to fail when we walk by faith in the light of His Word. We only fail when we make decisions without applying the principles of Scriptures.

Some of us are so afraid that if we trust God, He will lead us into something we can't do or face. How absurd! What kind of God would He be to play games with His children whom He loves? God gives us the strength and wisdom to deal effectively with every situation. Our problem is that we keep our eyes upon ourselves instead of looking to Jesus who is the Initiator and Completer of our faith. Hebrews 12:1, 2 says, "Let us also lay aside every weight, and sin . . . looking to Jesus the pioneer and perfecter of our faith."

It is no surprise that Jesus speaks so powerfully, yet gently, to the believers about anxiety (Matthew 6:25-34). The Christian has no reason to be anxious about the future. His choices which are in accord with scriptural principles are blessed by God Almighty. The Creator of the universe has promised to meet our needs. If God be for us, who can stand against us? God is committed to His beloved. When we doubt God's faithfulness to us, we may be greatly encouraged by reading Romans 8:31-37. The Christian has a sure and steadfast anchor, for God has given us His promises and He cannot lie (Hebrews 6:13-20).

I believe that the final step of decision-making is a matter of relinquishment vs. control. For the Christian, the point of growth is that final step when the person says "Yes" to God and places the outcomes in God's hands. We strive for control and it is the outcomes or circumstances that we desire to control. Fortunately, these are completely out of our hands. Our anxiety is related to our inability to control the outcomes. Even in praying for God's guidance, our secret wish is that He would reveal the outcomes. We want to know what will happen and that is impossible. "We walk by faith, not by sight" (2 Cor. 5:7). We walk by faith without the knowledge of outcomes. That is relinquishment, letting go of our frantic attempts to guess at the possibilities and predict the outcomes. Faith says, "I'll let go because God is in control." It means to stop asking, "What if's" and to say, "I'll trust God." He loves me. That's all I really need to know in order to choose without anxiety.

As Roy Fairchild reminds us,

> Through prayer and corporate worship we are assured that any mistakes we make in our decisions are not the last word for our lives. God's grace is such that he can show men how missteps might be redeemend. We have all made mistakes and we will continue to make them. Some of our reactions may have seriously damaged our family and work relationships. We may have decided to act in a way that now seems to threaten our future. Yet God can take even these wrong decisions and say to us, "Behold, I make all things new" (Rev. 21:5). We know we cannot retrace our steps, but it may be that a way will be opened to us to join the highway at another point.[2]

George Sweeting, in a booklet entitled *Discovering the Will of God,* pointed out that indecision rather than wrong decisions is what defeats us. The Epistle of James emphasizes that the instability of indecision is like being tossed and driven by the wind. An individual who

2. Fairchild, *op. cit.*, p. 195.

vascillates because of doubt and unwillingness to trust God is unstable in all his ways. Only in making a choice do we discover the faithfulness of God.

I think sometimes our problem rests in not following carefully the directions God sets down for us in His word. An experience I once had illustrates this. A friend and I had decided to observe hawks migrating in western Pennsylvania and obtained meticulous directions from a local naturalist. The directions to the observation point were clear and complete. My friend and I journeyed easily until the last two-mile section. We noted that every detail of the directions to this point was accurate, even to the tenth of a mile. When we turned back the last road, however, we did not bother to note the odometer or measure the last two-mile distance. As we drove, the dirt road became rockier and steeper. In some places, it was scarcely suitable for a jeep, let alone a car. We passed two areas in which there was a field and a gas line but neither of those was a "T" junction, as had been indicated. After driving for what seemed a long time on the dirt road, we both agreed that surely we had gone far enough. Certainly the observation place could not be back that miserable road any further. So we turned around and concluded that our friend had given us erroneous directions.

We parked the car in one of the previous crossroads in a field. Three dirt roads led from that point. We spent the next 3½ hours climbing and scrambling over them. Nothing fit the description of the observation point as it had been given to us. Our feet were sore and blistered, we were sweaty and tired and angry. We complained to each other about the naturalist who couldn't give good directions. We spent the entire day fussing and fuming about his careless instructions to us. Finally, as it began to get dark, we returned to the car. We decided just for curiosity to measure the distance to the point where we had turned around. As the odometer clicked over to 1.9 miles my friend and I looked sheepishly at each other. We rounded a steep turn and went one more tenth of a mile. There, to our embarrassment, was the observation place just as plain as could be.

We had wasted an entire day because we didn't follow the directions clearly. The only basis for turning around was subjective. It didn't *feel* right on that bumpy road, and it seemed we had gone much further than we had. We had been hostile and angry at the naturalist for our mistake.

This experience illustrated for me how easy it is to make decisions on the basis of unsubstantial subjective hunches even when clear guidelines are provided. We distorted the directions, argued about the terms, complained about our predicament, and wasted a lot of energy. How often do we experience a similar thing when we fail to put faith in God's Word or trust the information He gives? The words of the song, "Oh what needless pain we bear," ring true when we fail to follow scriptural guidelines carefully.

One of the most outstanding Old Testament examples of a person who exemplified faith in God in the midst of an intense dilemma is King Jehoshaphat (2 Chronicles 20). The good king was surrounded by enemies ready to crush him. In prayer he petitioned God for deliverance, "O our God, wilt thou not execute judgment upon them? For we are powerless against this great multitude that is coming against us. We do not know what to do, but our eyes are upon thee" (2 Chronicles 20:12). Imagine how easily he could have been overwhelmed with fear. How many of us would have frantically tried to muster our forces for battle and take things into our own hands? But Jehoshaphat walked straight toward the enemy, sang praises to God, and gave thanks before any evidence from God that victory would come. He didn't try to hide or run away. Simply on the basis of God's promise, Jehoshaphat chose to face the enemy and claim victory. He was not given the details of the outcome in advance, but he knew that God was in control and the battle belonged to God.

Ask God to help you walk by faith and not by sight. Thank God for His control in the midst of difficult decisions. The only assurance You need to make good choices is to recognize and trust that God loves you and He gives you the victory. But you must be willing to step out and choose. Only then will you discover the beauty of God's faithfulness, and to your limited faith will be added still more faith.

David R. Leaman, Bedford, Pennsylvania, has been employed since 1975 by the Bedford-Somerset Mental Health/Mental Retardation Center. He serves as a psychological consultant, individual and family therapist, supervisor to student staff, and performs other related professional duties in the field of psychology.

His articles have appeared in *Counseling and Values* and in the *Personnel and Guidance Journal.*

Leaman received his EdD degree in counseling psychology and guidance from Ball State University, an MS degree in college counseling from Shippensburg State College, and the BA degree in psychology and biology from Wheaton College.

He holds active membership in the American Personnel and Guidance Association, the American Psychological Association, and the Christian Association for Psychological Services.

David and Joyce (Schwartz) Leaman are the parents of a young daughter, Shonelle Grace. They are members of the Bedford United Methodist Church.